DESIDERIUS
ERASMUS
WRITER AND CHRISTIAN HUMANIST

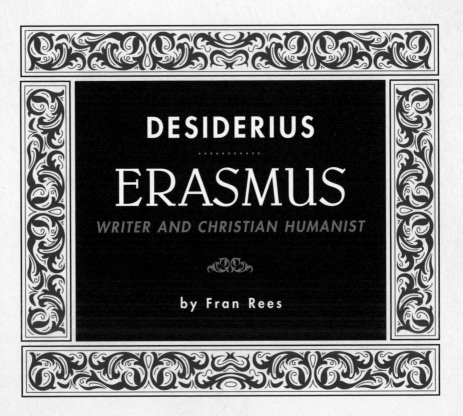

DESIDERIUS

ERASMUS

WRITER AND CHRISTIAN HUMANIST

by Fran Rees

Content Adviser: James F. Korthals,
Professor of Church History,
Wisconsin Lutheran Seminary

Reading Adviser: Rosemary G. Palmer, Ph.D.,
Department of Literacy, College of Education,
Boise State University

COMPASS POINT BOOKS ✦ MINNEAPOLIS, MINNESOTA

Compass Point Books
3109 West 50th Street, #115
Minneapolis, MN 55410

Visit Compass Point Books on the Internet at *www.compasspointbooks.com*
or e-mail your request to *custserv@compasspointbooks.com*

Editor: Sue Vander Hook
Page Production: Bobbie Nuytten
Photo Researcher: Svetlana Zhurkin
Cartographer: XNR Productions, Inc.
Library Consultant: Kathleen Baxter

Art Director: Jaime Martens
Creative Director: Keith Griffin
Editorial Director: Carol Jones
Managing Editor: Catherine Neitge

Library of Congress Cataloging-in-Publication Data
Rees, Fran
  Desiderius Erasmus: writer and Christian humanist / by Fran Rees
  p. cm—(Signature lives)
  Includes bibliographical references and index.
ISBN 0-7565-1584-X (hardcover)
  1. Erasmus, Desiderius, d. 1536. 2. Church history—16th century.
3. Humanists—Netherlands—Biography. I. Title. II. series.
  BR350.E7R38 2006
  199'.492—dc22   2005025096

REFORMATION ERA

The winds of change howled through Europe during the 1500s. The continent that had been united by the Catholic Church found itself in an uproar. In an attempt to reform the church, some people left the established religion, while others worked from within. The changes that began in Germany in 1517 when Martin Luther wrote his *Ninety-Five Theses* would transform everything. The Protestant Reformation's impact would be felt in all aspects of life—at home, in government, and in economics. Straddling the Middle Ages and the Renaissance, the Protestant Reformation would change the church, religion, and the world itself.

Table of Contents

1 BIG HOPES AND DREAMS

❧❀❧

In 1483, tragedy struck the town of Deventer in the Netherlands. Many people came down with a fever and swollen glands, and their skin turned a blackish tint. Then they died. Thirteen-year-old Desiderius Erasmus escaped the disease, but his mother didn't. She was one of the many victims of the bubonic plague—the Black Death, as it was called.

For more than a century, the plague had killed millions of people. One-third of Europe's population had already died from the deadly disease. Now it had struck Desiderius' family.

Something else was also complicating his life. Desiderius and his older brother Pieter had lived with their mother because their mother and father had never married. Society looked down on children of parents

A doctor and his assistants take care of a victim of the plague.

The first outbreak of the bubonic plague occurred in China in the 1330s. Since China was a busy center for world trade, it was only a matter of time before traveling merchants spread the disease to western Asia and Europe. In 1347, the disease hit Italy, killing people with terrible speed. Within a year, it reached England, where people began calling it the Black Death because of black spots that appeared on the skin. For five years, the disease traveled rapidly throughout Europe, killing about 25 million people—one-third of Europe's population.

who didn't marry. Desiderius often was embarrassed about his past. To make matters worse, his father had been a Catholic priest, and priests were not allowed to marry or have children. A child of a priest was considered a nonperson, someone who had no place in society.

After their mother died, Desiderius and Pieter were alone. They continued to go to the School of St. Lebwin, but then students started coming down with the plague. The school closed its doors. There was no reason for the boys to stay there and possibly catch the disease.

They went to live with their father about 100 miles (160 kilometers) away in Rotterdam. But within a year, tragedy struck again. The boys' father also died of the plague. Now Desiderius and Pieter were orphans.

Shaken and confused by his double tragedy, Desiderius had to face the world without parents. He was helpless and unsure of himself. But he had big hopes and dreams—he wanted to attend a university, study literature, and write. From the time he was very young, he enjoyed reading, writing, and creating poetry. At school he learned to speak and write in Latin, which allowed him to read the ancient literature of Greece and Rome. He was a gifted student with a big appetite for knowledge. The world of learning became his life.

Since Desiderius and Pieter had no place to live, Peter Winkel, a teacher at their Rotterdam school, agreed to take care of them. Winkel didn't recognize what a talented writer and student Desiderius was. He didn't know about his love for literature and his strong desire to go to school. His main concern was how to take care of two children.

Catholic monks shaved their heads, except for a narrow horizontal band of hair.

Winkel's solution was to send them to a monastery, a place where Catholic monks lived to fulfill their religious vows. There they would be taken care of and receive a proper education. Winkel arranged for the boys to attend the monastery of the Brethren of the Common Life at Bois-le-Duc in 's-Hertogenbosch, the Netherlands.

Desiderius was not happy there, and he saw his dream of attending a university fading away. He didn't want to become a monk and thought he was wasting his time at the monastery. However, the brothers had no choice but to stay. Three years later, they finished their education, but Winkel insisted they go to yet another monastery. There was still no money to support them and no place for them to live.

Desiderius was hurt and angry. Other poor young men went to a university. Why couldn't he? Bravely, he approached Winkel and boldly declared he would not go to another monastery. He was going to Italy. Desiderius argued bitterly with Winkel about this, but in the end, Desiderius had no choice but to go to the monastery. After all, it took money to travel to Italy, and he had none.

At about the age of 16, Desiderius entered the monastery in Steyn, the Netherlands. For the next five years, he and his brother lived and studied with the monks. Life was not all bad for Desiderius. The monks gave him special freedoms because he was not physically strong and his stomach was easily upset. Sometimes they pretended not to notice when he didn't attend religious services.

Still, Desiderius was not happy. Not wanting anyone to know how angry he was inside, he used his charm and intelligence to impress his teachers. Some

Monks spent many hours a day studying the Bible and church law.

of them recognized that he was a special student with extraordinary abilities. People outside the monastery were even hearing about this talented young man.

But not everyone at the monastery understood Desiderius. One of his superiors accused him of being lazy and ordered him to put down his books and pen. Desiderius complained in letters to his friends that he

13

was being forced to rot in idleness. He took revenge and wrote an article titled "Against the Barbarians," criticizing the leaders of the monastery—or the barbarians, as he called them. One of his superiors then gave him a remarkable opportunity. A Catholic bishop needed a secretary, and Desiderius applied for and got the job. Without hesitation, he packed his bags and left the monastery. Perhaps now he could fulfill his hopes and ambitions.

Desiderius vowed to rise above his tragedies and his poverty. He ventured into the world hoping to become what he wanted to be—a writer and a scholar. The road ahead would not be an easy one, but never again would he set aside his books or pen.

Desiderius Erasmus would one day rise to fame. Kings and emperors would honor him and invite him to live among them. Other people in high places would compete for his attention to improve their reputations. Common people all over Europe would read his writings and follow his teachings.

Leaders of the Catholic Church would also come to admire Erasmus. Although he criticized the church in his writings, he wouldn't split away from it as others did during the time that came to be called the Protestant Reformation. He wanted the church to change, but he didn't want people to leave and start a new church. Erasmus pointed his readers to what he believed was the worthy life. He encouraged them to

Desiderius Erasmus spent most of his time writing books and letters.

improve their character and follow the example and teachings of Jesus Christ.

Erasmus became one of the leading thinkers and the most famous scholar of his time. He was witty, charming, and intelligent, and always an independent thinker. His ideas became the foundation of a movement called humanism, which emphasized the development and perfection of the individual.

The books he wrote became best sellers, and he became a wealthy man. Desiderius Erasmus eventually fulfilled his dream—to write. ◈

2 *Chapter*
YOUNG ERASMUS

⤮

Much of Desiderius Erasmus' childhood is a mystery. Even the exact year of his birth is unknown. He was born on October 28, possibly in 1469, in Rotterdam, the Netherlands.

His father, Roger Gerard, a Catholic priest, worked for the church as a scribe. Day after day, his job was to make handwritten copies of books. Gerard had spent some time working in Italy, but his hometown was Rotterdam.

Desiderius lived with his mother, Margareta Boeckel, the daughter of a physician. His last name was not Gerard or Boeckel, however. He went by Erasmus, the Greek form of Gerard. Although his parents never married or lived together, both of them made decisions about their son.

As a child, Desiderius Erasmus sang in a boys' choir in Utrecht, the Netherlands.

Erasmus was born in this house in Rotterdam, the Netherlands, in about 1469.

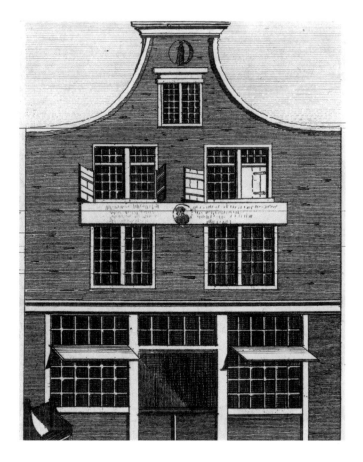

Desiderius Erasmus started school when he was 4 years old. When he was 9, he received musical training and sang in a boys' choir at the cathedral at Utrecht in the Netherlands. The next year, his father enrolled him and his older brother Pieter in the School of St. Lebwin in Deventer.

The school was an important center of learning in Europe. It taught Christian morals, daily devotion to God, and worship. It also trained students to live a Christian life. Students learned that the truly religious person was one who honored God, gave money to others, and lived humbly without a lot of worldly goods.

At the Deventer school, students followed a strict schedule that included fasts, vigils, reading, and prayer. Sometimes students were not allowed to speak, play, or joke for long periods of time.

Desiderius often complained about the school being too old-fashioned and about the poor teaching. Even so, he was a hard-working student who was talented and eager to learn. His hunger for knowledge was hard to satisfy. While most students were struggling to learn basic Latin, Desiderius already knew how to speak it and write it.

Knowing Latin made it possible for him to study the writings of some of the most scholarly and educated people. One of his teachers introduced him to ancient Greek and Roman literature. At last, he was challenged and inspired.

His intelligent mind soaked up the words written hundreds of years before. Desiderius was just one of many people in Europe to become more interested in literature, the arts, education, science, and ancient cultures.

Desiderius' opportunities at school ended abruptly, however, when his mother died of the bubonic plague in 1483. After his father died the following year, Desiderius got his education in monasteries, first at the Brethren at Bois-le-Duc, then at Steyn, the Netherlands.

Although life at the monasteries was rigid and disciplined, Desiderius managed to find a way to read books, study, write letters, and build friendships. Monasteries held some of the finest libraries in the world, and the library at Steyn was excellent.

Latin was the main language of Western Europe for hundreds of years. Its alphabet of 23 letters—there is no j, u, or w—became the basis for most modern alphabets. By the early 1500s, the Spanish, French, and Italian languages had developed from Latin. Many modern English words have their origins in the Latin language. For example, the word gravity comes from the Latin word gravis, which means heavy. The Roman Catholic Church still considers Latin its official language, although the language of the people has been allowed in most church services since the mid-1960s.

Desiderius spent hours reading, copying, and memorizing ancient literature. He read Virgil, Horace, Ovid, Cicero, Juvenal, Terence, and Quintilian. He devoted himself to studying these literary masters. In order to become an expert in Latin, he forced himself to speak and write only in that language.

Learning was his passion, and writing was his life. "The more I write, the more I wish to write," he noted. Writing came easily for Desiderius. In letters to his friends, he often poured out his heart, trying to overcome the loneliness he felt as an orphan in a new place. He confided his secrets and passions

Monks devoted themselves to study, prayer, and worship of God.

in his letters and valued correspondence between friends. "To send and receive letters is the sole means of uniting absent friends," he wrote.

Writing was also a way to pass the time during the long, boring days of rigid schedules. Daily chores were demanding, religious services were long, and the food was poor. Bells rang throughout the night and day, calling the monks to their endless rounds of tasks, prayers, and religious duties. Erasmus had a

Monasteries were isolated from society so monks could fulfill their vows alone with God.

weak body and an independent spirit, which made it difficult for him to live the monk's life. He desperately wanted freedom to read, study, and write.

Because of his exceptional interests and talents,

his superiors finally gave him an opportunity to leave the monastery. In 1493, Desiderius Erasmus was hired as the secretary for Hendrik of Bergen, bishop of Cambrai, France. Erasmus walked out of the monastery, never to live there again. But before he left, he was ordained, or officially appointed, a Catholic priest, even though he didn't intend to practice as one.

Erasmus' duties as Bishop Hendrik's secretary fit him perfectly. His job was to write letters to powerful people, such as the pope and cardinals of the Catholic Church. Hendrik also wanted Erasmus to go with him to Rome, the center of the Catholic Church. Erasmus was excited to finally visit Italy, the land of scholars and new ideas.

The trip, however, was canceled. The bishop had hoped to be promoted to cardinal, a position just under the pope, the head of the Catholic Church. But he didn't get the position, and he and Erasmus settled in Brussels, Belgium. Erasmus' hopes were crushed.

When the bishop realized how

Today, the center of the Roman Catholic Church is still in Rome, Italy. In 1929, Roman Catholicism was granted special status in Italy. Its main facility was called Vatican City, the smallest independent state in the world. It has its own post office, supermarket, bank, railway station, electric plant, and publishing house. It is the home of the pope and site of the famous St. Peter's Basilica and the Sistine Chapel. The basilica was built over the supposed site of the tomb of St. Peter.

unhappy Erasmus was, he took away some of his duties so he could study. Erasmus now had time to visit libraries and read books. At the library in nearby Zonia, he discovered the works of St. Augustine. He lost himself in the writings of this famous religious writer and thinker.

By working for the bishop, Erasmus made a living and still had time to learn. He also had his first taste of being around powerful people. Hendrik was a member of the Regency Council for Archduke Philip the Fair, who would one day become king of Spain. The bishop took Erasmus with him on his visits to the royal court in Brussels. There Erasmus saw firsthand what royal court life was like.

Before the printing press, libraries contained only handwritten copies of books.

Much of royal life annoyed Erasmus. He thought important matters were overshadowed by petty

conversations and jealousies of the courtiers. He grew tired of everyone competing for the attention of royalty.

Reading and learning were still most important to Erasmus. He continued to write long letters to friends, casual acquaintances, and even people he had never met. He studied Greek and Latin, and tried to apply the wisdom of ancient writers to modern life. Scholars throughout Europe spoke and read only in Latin. It was the most acceptable way for scholars to communicate their ideas.

While working for Hendrik, Erasmus met a man named James Batt, who also loved ancient classical literature. Once Batt learned about Erasmus' talents and interests, he begged the bishop to let Erasmus attend the university in Paris. Batt thought Erasmus should work for a doctorate in theology, the study of religion. The bishop agreed to let Erasmus go. In the fall of 1495, Erasmus enrolled at the College de Montaigu in Paris, a university for scholars with little money.

Conditions at the college were very difficult. Students had to do their own washing, cooking, and scrubbing. They ate their first meal of the day at 11 A.M., when they received bread, a small pat of butter, some stewed fruit, vegetables, a small fish, and two eggs that were sometimes rotten. Students were expected to obey the rules, and those who

Bartolus de Saxoferrato.

A typical classroom in the 1500s

misbehaved were beaten, often until they bled.

Erasmus later wrote that the beatings at the university were savage. The buildings they lived in were falling apart, and many students became ill from bad food and unsanitary conditions. By the end of the first year, Erasmus came down with malaria. He spent the summer back at Hendrik's home to recover and build up his strength.

The following school year, Erasmus returned to Paris, but this time he lived in a private home. Someone, perhaps the bishop, gave him money to help pay for his room and food. Now he could continue his studies. But he was not always happy with his education. Often he was critical of his teachers and the narrow-minded material he was forced to learn. He wanted to express his own ideas and debate them with scholars.

Money was also a problem. People from Hendrik's hometown of Bergen, Norway, sometimes sent him money, but it was soon gone. To earn more, Erasmus tutored young students in Latin. But since he was not very healthy, sickness often kept him from working and making money.

In spite of his circumstances, he continued to write. He wrote letters to friends and worked on two books—*Antibarbarians* and *On the Art of Writing Letters*. He once wrote:

> *I am giving myself entirely to my books. I am bringing together scattered texts, and composing others, I allow myself no leisure but what my health permits me.*

It would be about 25 years before his books would be published. ◈

Chapter 3 — CHRISTIAN HUMANIST

❧∽❧

Europe was changing dramatically in the late 1490s when Erasmus was at the College de Montaigu in Paris. New ideas were quickly replacing the way people had thought and lived for hundreds of years. It was an era that would be known as the Renaissance.

At the university, the most important subject to study was God and religion. In addition to people's strong religious beliefs, some also believed in myths and superstitions. Mainly, religion was organized by the Catholic Church. From the time people were born until the day they died, church rituals and traditions were the center of their lives. Religion, politics, holidays, and social life all revolved around the church.

Common people learned about religion and God

A 16th-century illustration portrays theology as the top program of study at European universities.

from their priests, who taught from the Latin Vulgate Bible, the version used by the Catholic Church. Ordinary citizens did not have Bibles of their own. They couldn't read or speak Latin, so they depended on priests to tell them what the Bible said. Religious scholars, monks, and priests devoted their lives to studying the Bible, Latin, and laws of the church. They passed on their knowledge to people who attended church services. Some priests were better scholars and teachers than others, and some changed what the Bible said to fit their own beliefs. So what was taught to the people varied from priest to priest and from region to region.

The Catholic Church was not just a religious organization. It also had strong political power and could influence kings and princes. Royalty and empires came and went, but the Catholic Church had kept its authority over people and rulers for centuries. For the most part, the church made the laws, and political rulers carried them out. If someone spoke against the church or its leaders, church officials could declare that person a heretic, someone who disagreed with the laws or traditions of the church. They could then ask a secular, or nonchurch, official to try that person in court for heresy and carry out the punishment—often burning at the stake.

At the head of the Catholic Church was the

pope, who lived at the papal palace in Rome. He was assisted by cardinals, who were members of what was called the College of Cardinals. If a pope died, the cardinals selected a new pope, usually a member of their college. Next in rank were bishops, religious leaders who presided over geographical regions called dioceses. Then came priests, who led local churches. Each week, priests recited or sang religious services, held Mass, visited the sick and dying, and heard confessions of sinners.

Prisoners were sometimes tortured to persuade them to confess their crime of heresy, going against the Catholic Church.

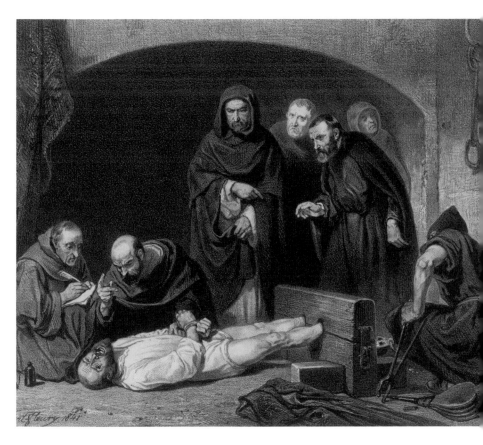

Most schools, like the one Erasmus attended as a boy in Deventer, were owned and operated by the Catholic Church. Students were taught religion, grammar, math, and other subjects. People who wanted to become religious scholars or leaders in the church took a religious vow, became a monk, and lived and studied in monasteries. Women who took religious vows lived in convents and became nuns. Monasteries and convents taught a strict form of religion and discouraged students from questioning ideas or looking for new ones. However, some church schools located in large city cathedrals were more open to new ideas. Some of them eventually became universities.

When Erasmus was growing up, some of the Catholic priests didn't set good examples of moral living. Priests took vows of celibacy, a promise to God that they would not marry. But some had relationships outside of marriage and had children. Society labeled the sons and daughters of priests as illegitimate, or illegal, and the

When Erasmus was a young adult, the head of the Catholic Church was Pope Alexander VI. He was the most powerful man in Rome and one of the most immoral popes to ever lead the church. His 11-year reign of corruption was characterized by greed, schemes, war, murder, and orgies. Alexander shocked the public with his personal lifestyle and his numerous mistresses who bore him many children. This climate of immorality no doubt set the stage for people like Erasmus and Martin Luther to openly criticize the Catholic Church.

Alexander VI reigned as pope of the Catholic Church from 1492 until his death in 1503.

church would not allow them to have normal jobs or careers. The church felt obligated, however, to offer these children jobs within the church. Erasmus was one of these children. He resented being the son of a priest, especially because it forced him into a career in the church—a career he did not want.

The Catholic Church had other problems, too. Local priests did not always carry out their responsibilities and sometimes didn't show up for church. Services and other religious ceremonies often were not being held. The Catholic Church also needed money to build and furnish church buildings throughout Europe. To raise money, the church encouraged people to buy indulgences, pieces of paper signed by the pope that promised forgiveness of sins.

With so many problems within the church, people began turning to nonreligious ideas. As early as the 1300s, many Italians were studying secular subjects and discovering more things about the world. By the late 1400s, this movement had spread to England, France, Germany, the Netherlands, Spain, and other

Catholic priests went from town to town selling indulgences, a document that promised for-giveness of sins.

countries. Scholars and artists of this era called the Renaissance began to write and create new ideas and beautiful art.

Renaissance thinkers studied people, cultures, history, poetry, public speaking, philosophy, language, and more. For many years, people had centered their thoughts on religion and life after death. Now many people focused their thinking on making their earthly life better. A central idea of the Renaissance was humanism, or the importance of human beings.

Erasmus believed in humanism, but he also had strong religious beliefs. With his mixture of old and new ideas, he came to be called a Christian humanist. He spent most of his waking hours studying and writing about these beliefs and ideas. He also wrote about problems in the Catholic Church. Although he supported the church and its teachings, he wanted the church to be better. He wanted it to reform—and change its ways. Later, he would discover just how controversial his ideas were. ✑

4 CITIZEN OF THE WORLD

Chapter

❦

When Erasmus finished his studies at the Paris university in 1496, he stayed in Paris to work as a teacher. In his spare time, he studied, wrote, and looked for a patron, someone who would support him financially. If he didn't have to make money teaching, he could devote his time to studying and writing.

When one possible patron decided not to support him, Erasmus was very discouraged. But another opportunity came his way. One of his pupils, Lord Mountjoy, invited him to go to England with him. Erasmus accepted the offer.

Now he could see and experience other places. The unwilling monk who had been confined to a monastery was now free to go wherever he wanted. His path would lead from one country to another. For

Engraving titled Erasmus With His Three Friends *shows Erasmus writing a book, an activity that filled most of his life.*

the rest of his life he never stayed in one place for more than a few years. He was comfortable moving around. Everywhere he went, he made new friendships and took part in lively scholarly discussions with many types of people. He was always learning new things from new friends, new countries, and new cultures. He fittingly called himself "a citizen of the world."

In 1499, Erasmus arrived in Cambridge, England, where he stayed for about a year. There he made many more friends and met scholarly people who helped him develop his ideas that combined humanism and Christianity.

Thomas More (1478–1535) was one of Erasmus' good friends, but he was an enemy to Reformation leaders like Martin Luther.

He also met Thomas More, a Renaissance thinker studying law in London. They became lifelong friends. Erasmus had finally met his intellectual match in More, who thought just as deeply as Erasmus. The two men spent numerous hours discussing a wide range of interesting subjects like peace, war, Christianity, God, mankind, and the universe. Erasmus also met some well-known religious men in England who agreed with his Christian humanist ideas. They appreciated his knowledge of literature, his many talents, his intellectual ability, and his religious beliefs. He was not looked down on for his poverty or his difficult beginnings. In fact, he became quite good friends with other humanists and scholars. He was soon accepted into London's high society.

One person he met was John Colet, a humanist and religious scholar. Colet influenced Erasmus' thinking and helped him understand the religious teachings of the day. The two men carried on lively arguments and often learned from each other.

Erasmus soon began to write down his key ideas and beliefs about Christian humanism. He explained his belief that Christianity and humanism were not separate ideas but actually supported each other.

John Colet (1466–1519) was one of Erasmus' best friends.

Thirty-year-old Erasmus was happier in England than he had been his entire life. He did not miss the drudgery of attending school and listening to boring teachers at the university. Here he was an equal with intelligent people who thought as he did. He made more lifelong friends and built a network of people that would grow and extend throughout Europe for many more years.

Friendships were very important to Erasmus. He once wrote:

Life without a friend I think no life, but rather death; ... I think nothing in this life to be preferable to friendship. ... Friendship is to be preferred to everything in the world; it is no less necessary than water, air or fire.

Except when he was working, Erasmus almost always made time for people, and he remained loyal to his closest friends. He kept in touch through letters—he loved the art of letter writing. During his lifetime, he wrote hundreds of letters to friends, religious leaders, and scholars.

Erasmus also wrote essays, poems, books, pamphlets, and translations. He and his pen were

The standard collection of Erasmus' letters is the 12-volume Opus epistolarum Des. Erasmu Roterodami in Latin. Few of Erasmus' original signed letters still exist. Most of them survive only in books that Erasmus published in his lifetime. He often organized the letters according to subject in order to make a point or support his beliefs. He wrote letters to many important people of his day, including King Henry VIII, Frederick the Wise of Saxony, Martin Luther, Thomas More, and Cardinal Thomas Wolsey.

Map shows present-day boundaries.

rarely separated. In his writings, he expressed his thoughts on almost every important subject of the day. He wrote about Christian life, classical literature, ancient wisdom, marriage, death, the church, war,

Erasmus never lived in one place very long. He moved from city to city in the Netherlands, Belgium, France, England, Italy, Germany, and Switzerland.

41

and countless other subjects.

Life as a writer, however, had many hardships. Erasmus constantly had to find patrons so he would have enough money for housing and food. When he didn't have a patron, he would find a job and work while he looked for other patrons.

Erasmus didn't like asking people for money. Perhaps one reason he kept moving from country to

Famous artist Hans Holbein, the Younger (1497–1543) drew three views of Erasmus' hands, one in the writing position.

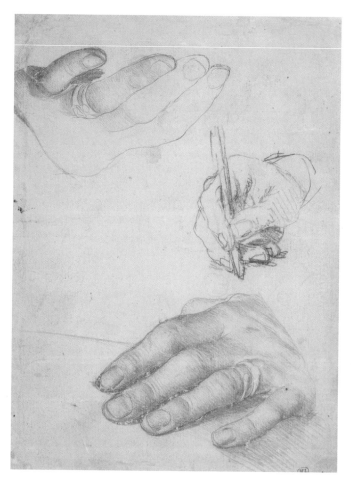

country was to avoid asking the same people for help time and again.

By the winter of 1499, Erasmus was in Cambridge and nearly out of money. He had recently received a considerable amount of support from the archbishop of London, but he didn't want to ask him for more. He felt he was begging, and he didn't like it. In a letter to Colet, he wrote:

> *But I ask you, what could be more shameless or abject [hopeless] than I, who have long been a-begging publicly in England?*

He told Colet about a friend who told him not to ask anyone for more money, but to "bear poverty bravely." Erasmus faced other hardships as well. He was frequently ill and described himself as frail. He was a sensitive person and reacted with strong emotions to events in his life. But he never stopped reading, studying, and writing. While he worked or traveled on horseback throughout Europe, he wrote down his thoughts and scribbled down notes. Sometimes he was so absorbed in his work that he forgot to eat or get enough rest.

In 1500, Erasmus decided to leave England and go back to Paris. His English friends gave him gold and silver coins so he could continue writing and find a printer to publish a book he was working on. As he was about to leave England, however, he ran into bad luck. Officials at the border took almost all his coins, claiming he couldn't take that much money out of the country. Neither he nor his friends knew about this rule. Erasmus was shocked, embarrassed, and downhearted. Now almost penniless, he traveled to Paris to look for people who would support him.

The printing press played an important part in Erasmus' success as a writer. Because his books could be mass-produced, many people read Erasmus' writings and knew who he was. By 1500, when he published his first edition of the Adages, print shops all over Europe were producing and distributing books faster than ever before. In just 50 years since Johannes Gutenberg developed the printing press, more than 10 million books had been printed. Without the printing press, only a few scholars may have read the writings of Erasmus.

In Paris, Erasmus finally found success as a writer. He published his first book—*Adages*—which made him a respected writer and established him as a humanist. The book looked like a little dictionary and contained 818 Greek sayings and proverbs. Short bits of advice included wise sayings such as:

> *War is sweet to those who do not know it.*
>
> *Kings and fools are born, not made.*

The *Adages* soon became a best seller, and Erasmus became known as an expert on ancient culture and literature. Eventually, 27 more editions were published, some of them with more than 4,000 proverbs and essays.

The title page of Erasmus' book, the Adages, *includes a portrait of the author and his own handwriting in a decorative layout.*

People all over Europe became interested in classical literature because of the *Adages*. The book became a standard reading and a reference for important writers like François Rabelais of France, Miguel de Cervantes of Spain, and William Shakespeare of England. Today, people use quotations from Shakespeare without knowing they were borrowed from Erasmus, who, in turn, took them from the ancient classics. The proverbs were very old, but as Erasmus wrote, "Proverbs improve with age exactly as wines do."

The *Adages* was filled with advice on life and death and thoughts on being human. One of them declared:

> *If you cannot play the role of a cow, content yourself with the role of the donkey.*

Then Erasmus elaborated on the proverb:

> *If you cannot do what you want to, do what you can. If fortune has not fulfilled you, take a good part of what is yours. If you cannot gain what you desire, occupy yourself with what is within your reach.*

Although Erasmus was enjoying success in Paris, he was forced to leave after six months. People were coming down with the bubonic plague, and Erasmus found himself fleeing the Black Death that once had taken his parents from him. He went back to his homeland, the Netherlands, where he continued to write. But this time, he wrote a book about religious matters.

In 1503, he published *Enchiridion Militis Christiani (Handbook of a Christian Soldier)*. This book encouraged the Catholic Church to change and improve its ways. At first, the book didn't make much of a stir. But 10 years later when criticism of the church was growing throughout Europe, it became very popular.

In 1505, Erasmus was once again in England, where he stayed for the next year and a half. There he renewed friendships with people like More, Colet, and Lord Mountjoy. He moved from place to place in London, staying at the homes of friends and making new friends along the way.

Erasmus gave a special gift to one of his friends, William Warham, the Archbishop of Canterbury. It

Erasmus dedicated one of his books to William Warham, the archbishop of Canterbury.

was his translation of a Greek work called *Hecuba*, by Euripides. Warham was so grateful that he called Erasmus aside and quietly gave him a gift of money. Erasmus later told his friend, William Grocyn, that it was a huge sum. Grocyn laughed and said Warham probably gave him money so he would dedicate the book to him when it was published. Grocyn's comment must not have bothered Erasmus, because he dedicated the book to Warham when it was printed.

Erasmus often dedicated books to people to show his gratitude for their generosity and character. He flattered Archduke Philip of Austria when he dedicated a book to him—*Erasmus: The Education of a Christian Prince With the Panegyric for Archduke Philip of Austria*. Because Erasmus was such a popular writer, his dedications helped make others famous. Sometimes people rewarded him with money, but other times they just appreciated what he did.

Becoming famous didn't end Erasmus' worries over money, however. Some publishers were honest and gave him copies of his books to sell or give as gifts. But sometimes he didn't get paid for his published works. Other times, dishonest publishers would steal copies of his manuscripts, print them, and sell them without paying him. The business of publishing and printing was still new at the time, and laws didn't exist to protect writers from dishonest people or publishers.

At times, Erasmus didn't have the physical strength to keep up with his writing. During his stay in England, at about the age of 36, he was feeling worn out from his continual studies and travels. He wrote:

> *Life at best is fleeting. I have decided to be content with my mediocrity ... and to devote the rest of my days to preparation and meditation on death.*

However, he didn't stop working or writing. He was about to realize one of his lifelong dreams—a visit to Rome. ✍

Erasmus was not a physically strong person, and sometimes illness made it difficult for him to write.

Chapter
5 ITALY AND THE HOLY CITY

⮜⛬⮞

In 1506, Erasmus was on his way to Italy. He was especially eager to see Rome, the place people called the Holy City. He had been hired to accompany two young men there—the sons of the doctor to the king of England—where they would attend school. He fulfilled his obligation and wound up staying in Italy for three years.

He went to libraries, studied Greek, visited the center of the Catholic Church, and talked with scholars. He enjoyed being in the country where ancient writers had lived and written their famous works. Erasmus wrote:

> *I came to Italy mainly in order to learn Greek. ... To Italy alone I have journeyed of my own free will, partly to pay at least*

Pope Julius II hired famous artists Bramante, Michelangelo, and Raphael to work for him in Rome, Italy.

*one visit to her holy places, partly to profit
from the libraries of that part of the world,
and make the acquaintance of its men of
learning.*

For a while, Erasmus stayed in Venice, Italy, at the home of a printer named Aldus Manutius. While Erasmus was there, Manutius published a larger edition of the *Adages*. This version contained Erasmus' notes and essays on the proverbs. It made Erasmus the most famous interpreter of the classics in Europe. Through his writings he became a mentor, or teacher and example, to his readers who received guidance for living and thinking from his book.

In February 1509, Erasmus finally visited the papal palace in Rome. Since he was still a priest, many leaders and religious dignitaries of the Catholic Church greeted him warmly. One of them was Cardinal Giovanni de Medici, who would become Pope Leo X four years later.

Erasmus was honored by how well Catholic leaders treated him. At the same time, he was surprised

When Erasmus visited Rome, Italy, in 1509, Pope Julius II was head of the Catholic Church. Julius' major accomplishments were his support and advancement of art, literature, and archi-tecture. In 1506, he started construction of St. Peter's Basilica in Rome, possibly the largest Christian church in the world, with a capacity of more than 60,000 people. The pope hired art-ist Michelangelo to paint the now-famous ceiling of the Sistine Chapel just north of St. Peter's.

and disappointed in the pomp and ceremony of the Catholic Church. He was not comfortable with the luxurious clothing that church leaders wore, nor did he like their lavish rituals. Erasmus thought Pope Julius II acted kingly. He also thought his sermons were uninteresting.

It shocked Erasmus to see hordes of employees, servants, and guards surrounding high-ranking church leaders as though they were royalty. Erasmus didn't keep his thoughts about church leaders to himself. He often spoke out and wrote openly about how he felt. What he thought about the church was no secret.

When Erasmus decided to leave Rome, he shared with a friend one reason he was not impressed with

The pope, a cardinal, and two bishops in some of the ornate clothing worn by leaders of the Roman Catholic Church

church leaders. It had to do with a visit he had made to Cardinal Grimani, one of the top officials of the church. Arriving at the papal palace, Erasmus had asked to see Grimani. The servant told him the cardinal could not see him because he was visiting with noblemen. But when Erasmus gave his name, the servant hurried in to the cardinal and came back quickly. The cardinal would see him. Erasmus was disappointed that the cardinal wouldn't see him when he was an unknown person. He didn't like it that he had time only for famous people.

Erasmus and Grimani visited for two hours, and the cardinal asked Erasmus not to leave Rome. He invited him to stay at his home and enjoy his fortunes and his wonderful library filled with books in many languages. Erasmus later told his friend:

> *If I should happen to have known this man at another time, I should never leave the City. ... But I had already decided to leave, and ... it was hardly right to stay there.*

The cardinal assured Erasmus that his invitation came from his heart and begged him not to judge him by the behavior of his servant. He asked Erasmus to visit him again before he left Rome. However, Erasmus didn't go back to see Grimani. He was afraid he would be tempted to accept the cardinal's generous offer.

The pope and his cardinals met to talk with people in the Sistine Chapel.

It would be a life of luxury and he would no longer have to worry about having enough money. But it was a lifestyle that went against his beliefs. He had much inner conflict over his decision to leave Rome. "My mind was never so bad to me," he said. For the principles he so strongly believed in, he gave up a chance to live without financial worries. But the religious and moral standards he believed in were more important to him.

Erasmus also wanted to leave Italy to get away from prejudice. He liked Italy's simple lifestyle and the gentleness of the common people, but he didn't like the way many people looked down on foreigners. He didn't believe people should be prejudiced against anyone.

Erasmus had made his decision, and he regretfully left Italy to return to England. He left behind one of his dreams—to be in Rome, the Holy City and the place where he had wanted to live. But he looked back on his time there with fond memories.

Erasmus traveled through the Swiss Alps on his trip back to England. He may have passed through this walled town of Coire.

Later he wrote:

> *A deep regret for Rome is inescapable, when I think of its great store of great advantages available together. First of all the bright light, the noble setting of the most famous city in the world, the delightful freedom, the many richly furnished libraries, the sweet society of all those great scholars, all the literary conversations, all the monuments of antiquity ... gathered together in one place.*

Erasmus now started his journey back to England, a country he considered his second homeland. Even as he traveled, he continued to write.

On the back of his horse as he trekked through the Alps, he wrote down his ideas for his new work—*The Praise of Folly*—the book that would make him even more famous. ॐ

Chapter
6 SPEAKING HIS MIND

❧⟨✕⟩❧

Erasmus arrived again in London in 1509, where he stayed at the home of his friend Thomas More. He quickly settled down to write.

In just a few days, he finished *The Praise of Folly*, a satire in which Erasmus flipped things upside down and poked fun at everything that had to do with humankind. In it were ideas that were very important to him—humanism, Christian commitment, and pacifism. The book was an immediate success. People of all walks of life read it and enjoyed its mocking tone. It also contained good advice—live from the heart with compassion toward all people. Erasmus didn't consider it a masterpiece, but for many years it was a very popular book.

People particularly liked Folly, the main character,

who made fun of society. He spoke out against people in positions of authority. No one escaped Folly's attack—theologians, monks, cardinals, the pope, the king, and courtiers. According to Folly, monks do not live like Christ, and bishops are more concerned about money than Christian character. Cardinals put ambition, wealth, and prestige above inner riches, Folly declared. Popes glory in war rather than in the cross of Jesus Christ, he said.

Erasmus didn't hold back his attacks against the Catholic Church. He revealed what he believed to be corruption in religion and asked church leaders to change their ways and reform the church. Religious leaders were not the only people Erasmus ridiculed. He also made fun of princes, philosophers, and writers.

The Praise of Folly admired what Erasmus called the wise foolishness of a genuine Christian—living the Christian life seemed impractical, but it was the smart way to live. He portrayed the Christian life as a kind of divine madness. Fools for Christ, as he called Christians, become "good fools" for the sake of Christ. The true Christian, he said, senses the supreme goodness of God, experiences a flight of the spirit, and gets a taste of heaven.

Shouldn't you give up wealth, power, and prestige for the sake of being a humble Christian, the book inquired. Erasmus claimed that people should embrace Christianity with their hearts rather than their minds. He asked his readers to consider Jesus and how he suffered the shame of dying on the cross.

Painting titled Christ Crucified *by artist Anthony van Dyck (1599–1641)*

Patience, humility, and compassion may appear foolish to the world, but they are the way of the true Christian, Erasmus taught.

Erasmus was now famous and highly respected as a writer and Christian humanist. His *Handbook of a Christian Soldier* was reprinted in 1509 and again in 1515. His book had become so popular that people formed groups to study it and tried to follow its message and teachings.

> *Erasmus taught that the Christian's battle was against three enemies: the flesh, the devil, and the world. He wrote that "all of those spooks and phantoms which come upon you as if you were in the very gorges of Hades [hell] must be deemed for naught [nothing]."*

In his *Handbook*, Erasmus explained what he thought a true Christian should be. He made clear that he believed a good Christian would experience spiritual warfare against the devil. A good Christian soldier, he said, has God on his side, but each person must do his or her part to fight off evil. He encouraged Christians to live a good life by imitating the example of Jesus Christ.

The Christian life was a spiritual battle, Erasmus said, and the battle took place within the heart. But the Christian had spiritual weapons to fight this battle, he said. The weapons were prayer and Bible study. He asked people to pray that their lives would improve.

He also asked his readers:

If you walk in the spirit, where are the fruits of the spirit? where is love?

German artist Albrecht Dürer was inspired by Erasmus' Handbook of a Christian Soldier *to make an engraving titled* Knight, Death, and the Devil.

Erasmus hoped all people would be like the Good Samaritan, the man described in the Bible who helped an injured man he found alongside the road.

where is joy? where peace toward all? where patience, long suffering, goodness, kindness, compassion, faith, modesty, continence, and chastity? Where is the image of Christ in your behavior?

Then he encouraged them:

May you then in kindness correct the erring, teach the ignorant, raise the fallen, console the despondent, aid the toiling, relieve the needy. In a word, let all your possessions, all your concern, all your care be directed toward the imitation of Christ.

Erasmus also cautioned Christians not to get lost in rituals and symbols of the church. He believed it was the attitude in which deeds were done that was important. Just going through church rituals and celebrating Mass didn't make a good Christian. He argued that a common person could be just as spiritual as a monk or a priest. Being a church leader did not automatically make a person a good Christian.

The *Handbook* was Erasmus' way of explaining the Bible and the message he wanted his readers to know. He believed each person—not just religious leaders—should be allowed to read the Holy Scriptures regularly to learn how to live day to day. He wrote that the New Testament, one part of the Bible, is the law of Christ and that Christians should obey its teachings and focus on inner beliefs.

Many religious leaders were upset with Erasmus' *Handbook*. They saw this kind of literature as a threat to the strict principles of Catholicism. Many years later, after Erasmus died, the Roman Catholic Church banned the *Handbook* because it criticized church rites, rituals, traditions, and practices that Erasmus called superstitions.

Studying ancient writers also went against the wishes and traditions of the Catholic Church. Because ancient writers lived before Jesus Christ was born, the church considered them pagans. Church leaders thought these writers might lead people away from the church and its teachings. This didn't bother Erasmus. He was both a humanist and a Christian. He saw how ancient writings and religious beliefs could come together into one package. The ancient writers often described the perfect person—someone who constantly tried to become better. Erasmus agreed with them and thought Jesus was the example of that perfect person.

Erasmus also criticized the way the Catholic Church handled confession. Why confess to a priest, he asked, when you can confess your sins directly to God? He taught that ordinary believers could live the highest form of a religious life.

Erasmus also believed that the Latin Vulgate translation of the Bible used by the Catholic Church was filled with errors—6,000 of them, he claimed. Erasmus thought people needed an accurate version of the Bible. The New Testament portion of the Bible was originally written in the Greek language. Erasmus collected, compared, and studied these Greek manuscripts to produce an edited version. In 1516, he finished a new edition of the Greek New Testament. He also included short essays and notes with his own ideas about the meaning of the text.

By publishing a Greek New Testament, Erasmus

gave scholars something to compare to the Latin Vulgate. In many ways, the Greek New Testament was different from the Vulgate. These differences led to criticism by the Catholic Church. But Erasmus hoped church leaders would be open to discussion. He wanted the church to change.

The title page of the Latin Vulgate Bible, the official Bible of the Roman Catholic Church

Having a readily available Greek New Testament provided a resource for people who wanted to make the New Testament available in the language of the people. In 1522, a German priest named Martin Luther finished translating the New Testament portion of

William Tyndale works on his translation of the Bible into the English language.

the Bible into German. Luther relied on Erasmus' Greek New Testament for much of his work on the translation.

William Tyndale (c. 1494–1536) , an English priest and scholar, translated the New Testament and parts of the Old Testament into English. For 11 years, he was hunted down by English authorities and officials of the Roman Catholic Church. Translating the Bible into any language except Latin was against the law and against the church. Tyndale moved from city to city to avoid arrest. Although hundreds of copies of his Bible were burned, he managed to smuggle thousands of copies into England on barges and boats. Finally, he was arrested and found guilty of heresy—going against the teachings of the church. In 1536 he was burned at the stake as punishment for his crime.

Erasmus had high hopes that the Catholic Church would listen to him and make some important reforms in the church. Many others in Europe also wanted changes in the church. Some of them were even more outspoken than Erasmus. 🐦

EX CAPITE XIII.

ET admirata eſt uniuerſa terra poſt beſtiam.) ϗ ἐθαυμάθηϗ ἐν ὅλη τῇ γῇ ὀπίσω τ̃ Θηρίου, id eſt admiratio fuit in tota terra poſt beſtiam. Qui in captiuitatē duxerat.) ἔιτις ἀιχμαλωσίαν συνάγῃ, ϗ ἐις ἀιχμαλωσίαν ὑπάγει.i.qui captiuitatē cōtrahit, in captiuitatē abit Laurentius ſecus legit. Characterem in dextra,) χάραγμα, id eſt notam impreſſam, ſiue in ſculptam.

EX CAPITE XIIII.

QVod mixtum eſt mero.) τοῦ κεκεραμένου ἀκράτου, ut mero ſit ablatiui caſus, & referatur ad uino.Nam Græcis κεράννυσθαι dicitur, quod infunditur in calicem bibituro,etiam ſi non diluatur aqua, aut alio potus genere.

Amodo iam dicit ſpiritus.) Græci ſic diſtinguūt, ut amodo ſit finis ſentētiæ, ut ſit ſenſus poſt hac fore beatos q̃ in dño fuerint mortui. Deinde ſequit̃ ναὶ λέγῃ τ̃ πνεῦμα.Etiam dicit ſpiritus. Et hic etiā confirmantis eſt. In lacum iræ dei.) ἐις ληνὸν, qui eſt lacus, in quem exprimitur uuarū liquor.

EX CAPITE XV.

QVia ſolus pius es.) ὅσιΘ Laurentius legit ἅγιΘ, id eſt ſanctus. Veſtiti lapide mundo & candido.) Græce eſt λίνον, id eſt lino mundo. Interpres legiſſe uidetur λίθον, quæ dictio una dūtaxat literula differt a lapide. Et ſplendido magis eſt q̃ candido, λαμπρὸν.

EX CAPITE XVI.

VVlnus ſæuū ac peſſimū.) κακὸν ϗ πονηρὸν.i.malū ac malū, græce eñ bis idē dixit, Niſi mauis miſerū ac malū. Qui es, & qui eras.) Quācħ interpres mutauit pſonam, tamē totidem ſyllabis dictum eſt, quibus ſuperius qui eſt, qui erat qui uenturus eſt, ὁ ὢν, ὁ ἦν, ὁ ἐρχόμενΘ. Etiā dñe.) ναὶ κύριε. Etiam cōfirmantis eſt. Grando magna ſicut talentū.) ὡς ταλαντιάια.i.talentaris & magnitudine talenti. Talentū magnum antiquis dicebatur, unde quicquid ingens eſſet, id ταλαντιᾶιον uocabant.

EX CAPITE XVII.

SVpra beſtiā coccineā.) κόκκινον, id eſt coccinā, purpurā regū indicans. Et hic eſt ſenſus.) ὧδε ὁ νοῦς.i.hæc eſt mens, ſiue intellectus.

EX CAPITE XVIII.

ET in delitijs fuit.) ϗ ἐστρηνίασε, Idē uerbū, quo cōpoſito uſus eſt Paulus in epiſtola ad Corinthios. Cū autem luxuriatæ fuerint in Chriſto uolūt nubere, de quo pluribus ſuo dictū eſt loco. Itē paulo poſt, ϗ στρηνιάσαντες.i. & laſciuierunt. Lignum tinium.) θύϊνον. Et ſimilæ.) ϗ σεμίδαλιν. Lapidē molarē magnū.) λίθον ὡς μύλον, id eſt lapidē tanɋ̃ molam. Hoc impetu mittetur.) οὕτως ὡρμήματι.i.ſic impetu mittetur.

EX CAPITE XIX.

QVaſi uocem magnā tubarū multarū.) ἤκουσα φωνὴν ὄχλου πολλοῦ.i.audiui uocem turbæ multæ. Proinde cōſentaneū eſt interpretē ſcripſiſſe turbæ nō tubarū. Alleluia.) Quod Hebræis ſonat, laudate dñm. Siquidē הללו laudate eſt יה dñs.Ea uox crebra eſt in pſalmis laudate dominum. Vide ne feceris.) ὅρα μὴ.i.uide ne.Feceris addidit interpres, quo magis explanaret ſententiam. Et calcat torcular uini.) ληνὸν, quod ante uertit lacū.

Gog & magog.) Accuſatiui caſus eſt utrūcħ & generis maſculini, quod articulus Græcus declarat τὸν γωγ ϗ τὸν μαγὼγ, ſiue pro hominibus accipiēda ſunt ſiue pro gente. Nec eſt congregabit, ſed συναγαγεῖν.i.ad congregandū, aut ut cōgreget eos. Porro eos nō refert ad angulos, aut gentes, ſed ad Gog & Magog. Ego ſum alpha & ω.) γέγονα τ̃ ἄλφα, ϗ τ̃ ω.Noſter codex conſentiebat cū uulgata horū temporū æditione.

Iaſpidi ſicut chryſtallū.) κρισαλλίζουϮ, id eſt Chryſtalliçanti, ut referā ad lapidem.

Qui nocet noceat.) ὁ ἀδικῶν id eſt qui male agit, ſiue qui iniuſtus. Et ad huc poſitum eſt pro amplius. Beati qui lauant ſtolas ſuas.) Longe aliud Græci.

7 HOPE FOR A GOLDEN AGE

With the success of his Greek New Testament and the fame it brought him, Erasmus was ecstatic. He hoped people would read the Bible and follow its teachings. In this Golden Age, as he called it, people would follow the ideals of Christianity and humanism. A new way of thinking would make his hard work, poverty, and hardships worthwhile.

In 1517, when Erasmus was about 48 years old, he shared his enthusiasm for the future with Pope Leo X. Part of his letter said:

> *This age of ours ... has good hopes of becoming an age of gold, if such a thing there ever were. For in this age, ... I foresee that three of its greatest blessings will be restored to the human race: that true*

Erasmus' New Testament was published in Greek with a new translation into Latin on the facing page.

Christian piety which in so many ways is now decayed, the study of the humanities ... and ... perpetual harmony of the Christian world.

In 1517, the year
Erasmus published his
Greek New Testament,
Martin Luther, a
German priest, wrote
down 95 criticisms
against the Catholic
Church. He nailed
them to the door of
Castle Church in
Wittenberg, Germany.
The church door
served as a kind of bul-
letin board to invite
discussion among
students and profes-
sors at the University
of Wittenberg. But
Luther's Ninety-Five
Theses, as they came
to be called, set off a
spark of reform and
revolution against the
Catholic Church that
no one could stop. Thus
began the Protestant
Reformation.

He told the pope that the Golden Age would be an age of peace. Erasmus had great hopes for the Christian world, and so did Leo. The pope had already celebrated this Golden Age when he rode triumphantly through his hometown of Florence, Italy. His fellow citizens rejoiced that one of their own was now head of the Catholic Church.

It was a huge, elaborate procession of chariots, decorated animals, and citizens in costumes. The last chariot represented the Golden Age with a huge globe of the world and a young boy covered entirely in gold.

When the pope left Florence, he began working toward peace with the king of Spain. Erasmus also encouraged peace. Throughout his writings, he often argued strongly against war. He wanted all of

Europe to be united.

At that time, Europe was made up of different kingdoms. Kings constantly sought to increase and protect their kingdoms and their power, and boundaries changed frequently. Wars and political battles were common. But Erasmus hoped that kingdoms could live together peaceably.

Erasmus urged religious and political leaders to settle disputes without bloodshed.

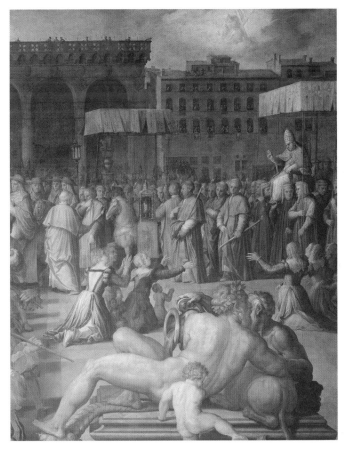

People celebrate the arrival of Pope Leo X in his hometown of Florence, Italy.

He wrote:

Let us look at the past 10 years. ... What region was not soaked in Christian blood? The cruelty of Christians surpasses that of pagans and beasts. We must look for peace by purging the very sources of war—false ambitions and evil desires. As long as individuals serve their own person[al] interests, the common good suffers.

During the Protestant Reformation, thousands of Europeans left the Roman Catholic Church. Because they protested against the church, they were called Protestants. Since Martin Luther sparked this mass movement, he was called the Father of the Protestant Reformation. His followers were called Lutherans. Today, about one out of four Christians in the world is a Protestant. About one out of six are Roman Catholic. Approximately one out of every five Protestants is a Lutheran, the name for one of many Protestant churches.

His golden age would see a return to basic Christian ideals. The corruptions of the Catholic Church would end, and the church would be unified.

Erasmus' writings inspired people to question and challenge the Catholic Church. Martin Luther read Erasmus' works and became the most significant leader of a movement that came to be called the Protestant Reformation.

Even though Erasmus and Luther would argue bitterly over some issues, they shared many concerns about the Catholic Church. Both were priests and wanted to reform the church. Like Erasmus, Luther did not want to destroy the church. But eventually, he split from it, as did many of his followers, who called themselves Lutherans—followers of Luther.

It has been said that Erasmus laid the egg that Luther hatched. His ideas and writings certainly

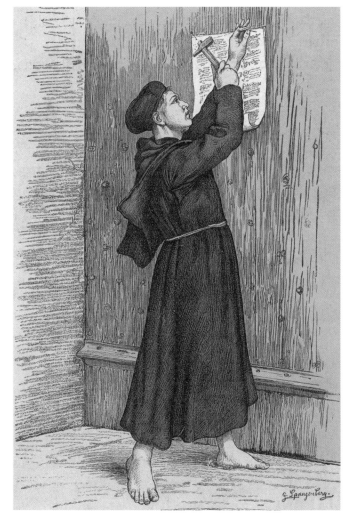

Martin Luther nailed his Ninety-Five Theses to the door of Castle Church in Wittenberg, Germany, on October 31, 1517.

encouraged Luther to think about changes that needed to be made in the Catholic Church. Erasmus helped lay the foundation for the Protestant Reformation, but he didn't do it intentionally.

Many people embraced Erasmus' ideas that the Catholic Church needed to change. But when the church did not change, they became determined to

Erasmus' writings helped spark the Protestant Reformation, a religious movement that spread throughout Europe.

break away from it.

The Protestant Reformation lasted many years. Arguing, fighting, bloodshed, and disharmony upset religion during this period. In the end, the Catholic Church would never be the same. It would no longer be the central church, and many other churches would be established.

The Protestants did not agree among themselves, either, and they formed many religious groups— Lutherans, Calvinists, Anabaptists, and others. The results of the Reformation affected all of Europe and eventually the world. It split the Catholic Church and created a clear distinction between Roman Catholics and Protestants.

Discouraged by the Reformation, Erasmus saw his hopes for the Golden Age fading. He declared in 1521 that his era was the worst since Christianity began 15 centuries before. He believed it would have been better to keep the Catholic Church with its problems than to seriously injure it. ❧

8 IN THE MIDDLE OF CONFLICT

❧❀❧

As the conflict between the Catholic Church and reformers continued, both groups pressured Erasmus to take sides. After all, he was the most famous thinker and humanist of the time and a well-known Christian. His ideas and writings had caused people to think about how the church and its leaders needed to change. Yet he was still a strong supporter of the church. Both sides wanted this popular and much-respected man on their side.

Erasmus, however, would not take sides. He and others such as John Colet continued to write about problems in the church. But they still remained loyal to Catholicism. Many church leaders admired them for that.

As time went on, however, people like Martin

Erasmus shakes hands with his printer, Johannes Froben, in Basel, Switzerland.

Luther spoke out even more against the church. As Luther became more well-known, his followers increased. Other religious groups also sprang up. Ulrich Zwingli of Switzerland, Martin Bucer of Germany, and John Calvin of France differed enough from Luther to have their own followers.

Followers of Protestant reformer John Calvin (1509–1564) came to be known as Calvinists.

Some church leaders asked Erasmus to condemn Luther and his ideas. But Erasmus refused because he agreed with Luther on many points. If he condemned Luther completely, he believed he would be supporting the Catholic Church's abuses and wrongdoings. If he approved of Luther completely, he would be joining a group that "contains many people with whom I would not want to have any business."

On March 28, 1519, Luther wrote his first letter to Erasmus, praising him as a scholar. Luther wanted Erasmus' support. Luther never got Erasmus' complete support, but Erasmus did encourage church officials to work with this outspoken reformer. He wanted them to correct him if he was wrong but not destroy him.

When church authorities spoke out against Luther, Erasmus wrote a letter to the archbishop in Germany:

> *I do not accuse Luther, I do not defend him.*
> *... If he is wrong, I would rather he were set*
> *right than destroyed; for this agrees better*
> *with the example Christ has given us.*

Even supporting Luther this much made some church leaders angry. Erasmus decided not to get himself "mixed up in civil strife" and would no longer write or speak for or against Luther. He even asked his printer to stop publishing Luther's works.

Erasmus tried to stay neutral while the debates and accu-sations between the Catholic Church and the reformers continued. Luther criticized Erasmus for being so cautious.

The teachings of Martin Luther (1483–1546) inspired the Protestant Reformation.

One of Luther's friends got involved in the conflict and attacked Erasmus strongly in writing.

Erasmus responded:

> *I love liberty. I neither wish to, nor can, serve any faction. ... it is not within me not to love peace and concord.*

Luther finally lost hope of gaining Erasmus' support. He wrote Erasmus saying he no longer expected anything of him but caution. What did it matter, Luther wrote, if he had one more enemy, since he had so many already, including the pope and the emperor?

Finally, Erasmus took a stand. He wrote *On the Freedom of the Will* to declare that he disagreed with Luther. Authorities of the Catholic Church were pleased that Erasmus had finally taken a stand, but many wished he had been harder on Luther.

Then Luther wrote a response to Erasmus. He accused Erasmus of being a hypocrite and an atheist, a man who didn't believe in God at all. The written debate between the two men continued for years. And their religious conflicts and arguments grew more heated.

Erasmus was living in the Netherlands at the time. The atmosphere there was becoming anti-Luther. Hundreds of Luther's books were burned. Arguments arose, some in favor of Luther and some against him.

*Many books
written by
Protestants were
burned during
the Reformation.*

Erasmus was becoming more disappointed with what was happening. Uncomfortable with the rising conflicts, he left the Netherlands in 1521 to go to Basel, Switzerland. Protestants and Catholics lived there, but the conflict had not become extreme.

Erasmus traveled on horseback through France and Germany, finally arriving 20 days later in Switzerland. There, he went back to his lifelong passion of writing letters. He published two books, one a collection of his letters and the other about letter writing. *Letters to Diverse Correspondants*

Basel, Switzerland, was one of Erasmus' favorite places to live.

included all the letters he had published so far plus 158 new ones—612 in all. There were letters to friends, patrons, printers, teachers, and powerful religious and political leaders. Over the next seven years in Basel, he published six volumes of his letters.

On the Writing of Letters was a book that taught others how to write a good letter in Latin. It explained that writing a letter was meant to be a mutual conversation between absent friends. He praised letters, saying:

For what subject cannot be committed to a letter? In them we feel joy, pain, hope, and fear. In them we give vent to anger, protest, flatter, complain, quarrel, declare war, ... relate, describe, praise and blame. In them we feel hatred, love and wonder; we discuss, bargain, revel, quibble, dream, and, in short, what do we not do?

The book became a success and was published more than 100 times.

With Erasmus' influence in Basel, the city soon became the center of humanism. Erasmus was now a rich man from the sale of his books, and he could spend his days writing. His opponents contin- ued to criticize him, some openly and others behind his back. Some said he was a coward for not taking sides in the Reformation. They pressured him to condemn Luther

Ulrich Zwingli (1484–1531) was the leader of the Reformation in Switzerland.

Ulrich Zwingli (1484–1531), the priest of Great Minster Church in Zurich, Switzerland, preached sermons that encouraged people to live strictly by what the Bible taught. He became the leader of the Protestant Reformation in Switzerland. Zwingli enjoyed Erasmus' writings, and when Erasmus finished his Greek edition of the New Testament, Zwingli made a hand-written copy of the entire text. Then he memorized large portions of it.

as a heretic who had gone against the teachings of the Catholic Church. Others went so far as to call Erasmus a heretic. Some even insisted he was responsible for the Protestant Reformation.

Erasmus answered these criticisms and accusations in letters and published writings. He refused to withdraw his opinions about the need for reform within the church. But he didn't have a solution for what should happen next, which left many people disappointed and angry. Erasmus often felt forced to explain and defend his earlier writings about the problems in the church. He softened some of his arguments, and some thought he was a coward for doing so.

By 1529, the conflicts of the Reformation reached Basel. On February 8, about 800 Protestants gathered and made several demands of the city council. When the council didn't reach a decision, the men took up weapons and invaded the central marketplace. The next day, the men stormed a Roman Catholic cathedral and began smashing and hacking at religious statues, paintings, and other

images. Erasmus thought the riot went too far, even though he sympathized somewhat with the rebels.

City officials then banned Catholic worship in Basel. Although Erasmus had enjoyed living in Basel for eight years, he decided it was time to leave. For the next six years, he lived in Freiburg, Germany, a city where most of the citizens were members of the Roman Catholic Church. ☙

The more radical Protestants destroyed religious images and Roman Catholic Churches throughout Europe.

87 ஒ

O · ERASMI · ROTERODA
· ALBERTO · DVRERO · AD
· EFFIGIEM · DELINIATA

ΤΗΝ · ΚΡΕΙΤΤΩ · ΤΑ · ΣΥΓΓΡΑΜ
ΜΑΤΑ · ΔΕΙΞΕΙ

M·D·XXVI·

Chapter
9 PREPARATION FOR DEATH

❧❦❧

Erasmus was about 60 years old when he went to Freiburg, Germany, in 1529. There he became very ill. Believing he was close to death, he worked hard to finish some of his writings. By now, many of his friends had died, including Thomas More, who was executed by order of King Henry VIII for not supporting the king's divorce from his first wife.

Eventually, Erasmus' illness forced him to stay in his room. But he didn't stop writing. In 1533, he wrote *Preparation for Death*, a small pamphlet in which he explained his deepest spiritual beliefs. This essay was mostly about death, but it was also what he believed about life. He filled its pages with practical advice.

Each day, Erasmus grew weaker. He was suffering

An engraving titled Erasmus of Rotterdam *by German artist Albrecht Dürer* physically, and he was saddened by the difficulties of old age. Often alone in his room, he recalled his youth, his friendships, and his many journeys across Europe. He read through his own books again and reflected on his life. Most of his friends had died, but he reread their letters, remembering his earlier, happier days.

Even though he was weak and ill, Erasmus longed to be in a larger and busier city than the small town of Freiburg. He wanted to return to Basel. He wasn't sure he could travel that far, and he wasn't sure Basel was a safe place. The conflicts of the Reformation were still going on there. But in May 1535, he bravely made the trip to Switzerland. He knew he would probably spend the last days of his life there.

That year, the Roman Catholic Church got a new pope—Paul III. The pope invited Erasmus to come to Rome and be part of a new council, perhaps a member of the College of Cardinals. The invitation flattered Erasmus, but he refused to return to Italy. He was not well, and he did not have the strength or the desire to work on projects that

During his reign from 1534 to 1549, Pope Paul III earnestly tried to correct the problems in the Roman Catholic Church. In 1536, he appointed nine members of the clergy to write a report on the Reformation and how the church could be restored. The report exposed serious abuses in the church and encouraged church officials to put a stop to them. However, the report was ignored, and no changes were made at that time.

involved religious argument or debate.

In February 1536, Erasmus wrote a will, a new version of one he had written long ago. He was now rich and famous and could leave generous gifts to others at his death. In his will, he gave his gold

Pope Paul III was the head of the Roman Catholic Church during the last two years of Erasmus' life.

91

watch to a friend. To others he gave other gold items, money, rings, clothing, household goods, medals, crosses, and other precious possessions. This was the last time Erasmus ever wrote.

Now too weak to write, Erasmus felt hopeless and defeated. After all, writing was his life. Praying gave him some hope and peace. On July 12, 1536, Erasmus uttered his last words—a prayer to God—and died. He was about 67 years old.

Students, friends, city officials, and members of the university in Basel attended his funeral. He was buried in the same church where reformers had destroyed religious statues and images seven years earlier.

Erasmus began his writing career with worthy ideas. He became the most famous scholar and thinker of his age. But he had no idea that what he was writing would spark a fire of change and bring about the Protestant Reformation.

During Erasmus' life, the demand for change spread rapidly throughout Europe, and no one could stop the wave of radical

While the Protestant Reformation spread throughout Europe, the Roman Catholic Church took steps to change. A movement called the Counter-Reformation spread to Catholic churches all over Europe. The church corrected many of its problems and tried to recover from the results of the Reformation. The Catholic Church also took measures to shield its members from Protestant beliefs by developing a list of forbidden books called the Index.

Erasmus is depicted as a heavenly symbol to be admired.

reform. In the midst of religious conflict, however, Erasmus fulfilled his dream to become a writer. He opened up people's minds to new ideas and

Many of Erasmus' books were burned after he died. Translations of the Bible in languages other than Latin were also burned.

encouraged individuals to live an admirable life. But he also became a controversial figure, even after his death. In 1543, seven years after Erasmus died, leaders of the Roman Catholic Church tried to prevent people from being influenced by his writings and ideas. They banned all of his works—no Catholic was allowed to read what he had written—and they burned many of his books.

Over the next 100 years or so, Protestants continued to read Erasmus' books, but his fame diminished. At the end of the 1600s, however, his works began to be read again. Many readers today still respect his works and regret that he was judged so harshly at the end of his life.

Erasmus wrote on subjects that are important to many people—Christian unity, an end to war, personal faith in God, and Christian conduct. Many people still share his beliefs and his hopes. However, most of them don't realize they came from Desiderius Erasmus—the man who came to be known as one of the first thinkers of the modern age and the prince of humanists. ♦

ERASMUS' LIFE

C. 1469

Born in Rotterdam,
the Netherlands

1478

Attends school
in Deventer, the
Netherlands

1465

1466

Johann Mentel
prints the first
German Bible

1473

Astronomer Nicolaus
Copernicus is born in
Torún, Poland

1474

Isabella becomes Queen
of Aragon; known as
the "First Lady of the
Renaissance"

WORLD EVENTS

1484
Becomes an orphan; attends school at 's-Hertogenbosch, the Netherlands

1487
Enters the monastery at Steyn, the Netherlands

1492
Becomes an ordained priest in the Catholic Church

1483

1483
Martin Luther, German Protestant Reformation leader, is born

1492
Ferdinand and Isabella of Spain finance the voyage of the Italian Christopher Columbus to the New World

ERASMUS' LIFE

1493

Becomes secretary to
Hendrik of Bergen,
the bishop of Cambrai

1495

Attends the College
of Montaigu in Paris

1495

1493

Maximilian I begins
reign as Holy Roman
Emperor

1495

Taino Indians on
Hispaniola stage an
organized attack on
the Spaniards, but it is
quickly crushed

WORLD EVENTS

1496
Works as a teacher

1500
Publishes first edition of the *Adages*

1503
Publishes *Enchiridion Militis Christiani (Handbook of a Christian Soldier)*

1500

1497
Vasco da Gama becomes the first western European to find a sea route to India

1503
Italian artist Leonardo da Vinci begins painting the *Mona Lisa*

ERASMUS' LIFE

1516

Finishes his edition of the Greek New Testament

1519

Begins debates with Martin Luther

1511

Publishes *The Praise of Folly*

1510

1517

Martin Luther posts his *Ninety-Five Theses* on the door of Castle Church in Wittenberg, beginning the Protestant Reformation in Germany

1513

Vasco Nuñez de Balboa is the first European to reach the Pacific Ocean

WORLD EVENTS

1521

Claims his own times are the worst since Christianity began

1529

Moves to Freiburg; writes *Preparation for Death*

1536

Dies in Basel, Switzerland, on July 12

1525

1524

German peasants rise up against their landlords in The Peasants' War, the greatest mass uprising in German history

1531

The "great comet," later called Halley's Comet, causes a wave of superstition

DATE OF BIRTH: c. 1469

NAME: Desiderius Erasmus

BIRTHPLACE: Rotterdam, the
Netherlands

FATHER: Roger Gerard

MOTHER: Margareta Boeckel

BROTHER: Pieter

EDUCATION: School of St. Lebwin at
Deventer, the Netherlands
Monastery of the
Brethren at Bois-le-Duc
Augustinian monastery at
Steyn
College de Montaigu in
Paris

DATE OF DEATH: July 12, 1536

PLACE OF BURIAL: Basel, Switzerland

FURTHER READING

MacDonald, Fiona. *The Reformation (Events & Outcomes)*. Austin, Texas: Raintree Steck-Vaughn, 2003.

Mullet, Michael A. *The Reformation*. Crystal Lake, Ill.: Rigby Interactive Library, 1996.

Reformation and Enlightenment: Stories in History, 1500–1800. Boston: McDougal Littell, 2001.

Saari, Peggy, and Aaron Saari, eds. *Renaissance & Reformation Almanac*. Detroit: UXL, 2002.

Shearer, Robert G. *Famous Men of the Renaissance and Reformation*. Lebanon, Tenn.: Greenleaf, 2000.

LOOK FOR MORE SIGNATURE LIVES BOOKS ABOUT THIS ERA:

Catherine de Medici: *The Power Behind the French Throne*
ISBN 0-7565-1581-5

Martin Luther: *Father of the Reformation*
ISBN 0-7565-1593-9

Pope Leo X: *Opponent of the Reformation*
ISBN 0-7565-1594-7

William Tyndale: *Bible Translator and Martyr*
ISBN 0-7565-1599-8

On the Web

For more information on *Desiderius Erasmus*, use FactHound.

1. Go to *www.facthound.com*
2. Type in a search word related to this book or this book ID: 075651584X
3. Click on the *Fetch It* button.

FactHound will find Web sites related to this book.

Historic Site

Erasmus Museum
31 rue de Chapitre
Brussels, Belgium 1070
+32 (02) 521-1383
Once the home of Erasmus, the museum houses his centuries-old portraits, medallions, and a cast of his skull

archbishop
Roman Catholic bishop of the highest rank who oversees churches in a large region

bishop
Roman Catholic leader in charge of a city or area

cardinals
officials of the Roman Catholic Church next in rank to the pope

classical
relating to ancient Greek and Roman cultures

court
the assembly of a king or queen and the high-ranking officers

courtiers
members of a royal court

dignitaries
people who hold positions of respect or honor

diocese
geogrphic area containing a number of churches under the authority of a bishop

fast
the practice of not eating food for a period of time

heresy
the crime of disagreeing with an accepted religious belief or tradition

Holy Scriptures
the Bible

humanism
a principle that emphasizes the development and perfection of the individual

hypocrite
person who puts on a false appearance

monastery
place where men live to fulfill their religious vows
and the promises they have made to God

monks
men who fulfill their vows to God in a monastery

New Testament
the second part of the Bible

ordained
appointed as a priest, minister, or rabbi

pacifism
the belief that fighting and war are wrong

patron
someone who supports an artist or writer

prejudice
hatred or unfair treatment of a group of people
who belong to a certain race or religion

proverbs
short sayings that express a truth or offer advice

reformers
people who urge or demand change

satire
literature that makes fun of human habits and
failures

theologians
experts in the study of religion

vigils
periods of time spent doing something through the
night such as watching, guarding, or praying

Chapter 2

Page 20, line 21: Léon E. Halkin. Translated by John Tonkin. *Erasmus: A Critical Biography*. Oxford: Blackwell Publishers, 1993, p. 6.

Page 21, line 2: Ibid., p. 6.

Page 27, line 13: Ibid., p. 27.

Chapter 4

Page 40, line 9: Ibid., pp. 6, 37.

Page 43, line 9: Ibid., p. 37.

Page 43, line 13: Ibid., p. 38.

Page 44, line 16: Ibid., p. 46.

Page 45, line 10: Ibid.

Page 46, lines 4, 7: Ibid., p. 68.

Page 49, line 9: Roland H. Bainton. *Erasmus of Christendom*. New York: Scribner, 1969, p. 74.

Chapter 5

Page 51, line 13: *Erasmus: A Critical Biography*, p. 65.

Page 54, line 17: Ibid., p. 70.

Page 55, line 5: Ibid., p. 72.

Page 57, line 2: Ibid.

Chapter 6

Page 63, line 2: Desiderius Erasmus. *Handbook of a Christian Soldier*. In Roland H. Bainton. *Erasmus of Christendom*. New York: Scribner, 1969, p. 70.

Page 64, line 7: Ibid.

Chapter 7

Page 71, line 11: *Erasmus: A Critical Biography*, p. 112.

Page 74, line 2: "The Roots of War." *U.S. Catholic* 68.5 (May 2003). Reproduced in *Biography Resource Center*. Farmington Hills, Mich.: Thomson Gale, 2005. http://0-galenet.galegroup.com.catalog.tempe.gov:80/servlet?BioRC.

Chapter 8

Page 80, line 22: *Erasmus: A Critical Biography*, p. 155.

Page 81, line 6: Ibid., p. 149.

Page 82, line 4: Ibid., p. 155.

Page 85, line 3: Ibid., p. 163.

Select Bibliography

Bainton, Roland H. *Erasmus of Christendom*. New York: Scribner, 1969.

Cameron, Euan. *Early Modern Europe: An Oxford History*. Oxford: Oxford University Press, 1999.

Collinson, Patrick. *The Reformation: A History*. New York: Modern Library Edition, 2004.

"Desiderius Erasmus." *Almanac of Famous People*, 8th ed., 2003. Reproduced in *Biography Resource Center*. Farmington Hills, Mich.: Thomson Gale, 2005. http://0-galenet.galegroup.com.catalog.tempe.gov:80/servlet/BioRC.

"Desiderius Erasmus." *World Eras, Vol. 1: European Renaissance and Reformation (1350-1600)*, 2001. Reproduced in *Biography Resource Center*. Farmington Hills, Mich.: Thomson Gale, 2005. http://0-galenet.galegroup.com. catalog.tempe.gov:80/servlet/BioRC.

Giles, Mary E. *Great Thinkers of the Western World*, New York: HarperCollins, 1999.

Halkin, Léon E. *Erasmus: A Critical Biography*. Translated by John Tonkin. Oxford: Blackwell Publishers, 1993.

Hildebrand, Hans Joachim. *The World of the Reformation*. New York: Scribner, 1973.

Lampe, G.W.H. *The Cambridge History of the Bible: The West, from the Fathers to the Reformation*. Cambridge: Cambridge University Press, 1969.

Lindberg, Carter. *The European Reformation*. Oxford: Blackwell Publishers, 2000.

MacCulloch, Diarmaid. *The Reformation*. New York: Viking, 2004.

Magill, Frank Northen. *Great Events from History*. Modern European Series. Englewood Cliffs, N.J.: Salem Press, 1973.

Pill, David H. *The English Reformation 1529-58*. Totawa, N.J.: Rowman and Littlefield, 1973.

Rabil Jr., Albert. "The Correspondence of Erasmus." *Renaissance Quarterly*, 48.3 (Autumn 1995): 657.

Renaissance, Volumes 6 and 8. Danbury, Conn.: Grolier Educational, 2002.

"The Roots of War." *U.S. Catholic* 68.5 (May 2003). Reproduced in *Biography Resource Center*. Farmington Hills, Mich.: Thomson Gale, 2005. http://0-galenet.galegroup.com.catalog.tempe.gov:80/servlet/BioRC.

Thompson, Stephen P., ed.. *The Reformation*. San Diego, Calif.: Greenhaven Press, 1999.

Fran Rees is the author of children's educational books and books on team leadership and group communication. She has taught English and music at the elementary and junior high school levels. She keeps extensive written and art journals of her life and interests. She lives in Mesa, Arizona, with her husband and daughter.

Image Credits